ROCHE RHYMES

and Other Verse

K. C. Phillipps

TABB HOUSE
Padstow

Dedicated to the memory of Trezaise Chapel
(1883-2001)

FOREWORD

The last notable collection of verse in the Cornish dialect appeared over sixty years ago, in 1933, and was called *A Cornish Collection*, by Bernard Moore. There are many good poems in that volume, but since then, for the most part, dialect verse now appears as single items: as entries in the Gorsedd verse competition, or published in small magazines, or broadcast on Radio Cornwall.

It amuses me that the least elitist, some would even say the least cultured, village in Cornwall, viz. Roche, should have become a centre of dialect verse. If Roche were in the USA, W. J. Hawken, before he died, might have been a cult figure, with students from far and near flocking to study dialect poetry, with the study of baseball thrown in for good measure perhaps. The very idea would have pleased Uncle Will, for he understood parody well.

More seriously, Uncle Will (I am entitled to call him this, since he was my mother's eldest brother) is a textbook illustration of the Latin dictum *poeta nascitur non fit*, a poet is born, not made. A few scraps of education in Roche school was all he had; then out as a kittle-boy to a claywork. Soon his powers of 'lowster' (hard work) earned him promotion. But from his schooldays, Uncle Will was handling metre and rhyme with flair and precision. Some of the family dismissed the whole thing as 'Will's nonsense'. It took him a lifetime to overcome this prejudice entirely, but for his eightieth birthday his family clubbed together to produce 'Shiner's Poems'. Shiner, meaning dandy, a dressy man, was his nickname.

Representing the next generation, and I fear one of the last with first-hand knowledge of the dialect, I make no apology for the title of this little book. 'Roche,' says the *Penguin Guide to Cornwall*, 'is an oasis of interest in a dreary district.' The interest for me, as will appear in these poems, is the people I knew in the village and the dialect they spoke, and at times still speak.

K. C. Phillipps
Mount, 1995

CONTENTS

THEY'M ALL GOIN'

We have words picked out from all the world that we are
    using now:
Bimbo, tycoon, lysteria, these words are all the go.
There are words from *Coronation Street*, and words from
    New York City,
But none picked out from our South-West; that really is a
    pity.

*   *   *

For they'm all goin', they'm all goin', the words we used to
    say,
Whether we want some *gurty meat*[1], or only a cup of tay,
Whether we just have *taties and point*[2], or p'raps a *piggy-
feast*[3].
They'm all goin', they'm all goin', the greatest and the
    least.

*   *   *

A well-known lady novelist, now alas no more,
Said Cornwall now is vanishing, compared to days of yore.
And one sign of disappearance, as I have heard it said,
Is our words will vanish with it and Cornwall will be dead.

*   *   *

For they'm all goin', they'm all goin', the words that some
    think funny:
Like *glaze*[4], in what be'ee glazin' at, and *gake*[5] and *glow*[6] and
    gunny[7].
Louster[8] won't be the word for work, nor *keenly*[9] for
    hardworking,
Nor shall we say 'You've got the *larr*'[10] if you're seen to be
    shirking.

1

The young say things are fab and great, and likewise also
    brill,
And these sound fine upon their lips; all well and good,
    but still,
When they're a bit more rational, they might say brave and
    good,
Or moderate words like *bravish*[11], but these won't be under
    stood.

             *   *   *

For they'm all goin', they'm all goin', they'm all goin',
    goin', gone.
We shan't express suspicion with 'What are 'ee on upon?'
We shan't express confusion with 'It looks like Launceston
    Jail',
And no one will know the difference between a *flasket*[12]
    and a *frail*.[13]

             *   *   *

Now to put to *quail*[14] is one thing, but a *quailaway's*[15] an-
    other;
And a girl who has been *forthy*[16] may perhaps not tell her
    mother;
But if she's *fore-right*[17], then perhaps she's not to blame.
But one thing must be obvious: these words aren't all the
    same.

             *   *   *

But they'm all going', they'm all goin', the words we used
    to know,
Like 'outward *flink*[17] and inward stink' when things are
    done for show.
Like 'goin' like a *skeiner*'[18], or 'goin' like the mail'[19],
Or 'looking like a *winnard*[20]' when we'm looking *wisht*[21]
    and pale.

             *   *   *

Are we proud, or far too humble, that we leave these words
    alone?
Do we want to keep them all shut up, used by ourselves
    alone?
Will those from upward think we are illiterate with no
    manners?
Do we fear they will despise us as a lot of country *janners*[22]?

*   *   *

For they'm all goin', they'm all goin', the words we used to
    use,
Whether we pick our feet up *fitty*[23], or *sluidge*[24] with our
    shoes.
And no-one will distinguish when we drink from when we
    gaddle[25],
And none will know just which is which, a *stiddle*[26] or a
    staddle[27].

*   *   *

Take a Scotsman, who will tell you how at times he takes a
    scunner,
And then explains the phrase to you, as if it was a wonder.
How may would explain to him 'Our dinner's all *zam-
zodden*'[28]?
But even if we use the word we make it sound half-rotten,

*   *   *

For they'm goin' up in smoke and *smeech*[29]; and soon
    there'll be no difference.
Most of the words that we still use are only here on
    suffrance.
'Tis 'What was father's word?' and 'What did mother used
    to say?'
And the memory of the dialect grows fainter every day.

If we could raise our consciousness that Cornish speech is
good,
If we could only use these words while they're still under-
stood,
We'd show the world we had a fine tradition still to follow,
We'd *scat*[30] 'em all to *flitters*[31], we'd up and beat 'em
hollow.

*   *   *

But they'm all goin', they'm all goin', the words we used to
like,
And we stand up and watch them, as if we can't blow nor
strike,
We'm watching of them disappear, by dozens and by
hunderds,
'Tis time, sure 'nough, I think, to stop 'em flowing down
the *cunderds*.[32]

*   *   *

And where's the records and the tapes to keep the memory
going?
And where's the books and articles? Without them there's
no knowing.
For while the Cornish language is in intensive care,
Research and cash for dialect just simply isn't there.

*   *   *

And they'm all goin', they'm all goin', the words we used
to like
When a pick-axe was a biddix and a hay-fork was a pike.
There won't be any Cornish words nor Cornish sayings
nuther;
For it will all have vanished into smeech and into smother.

*   *   *

4

1 meat made of pig's innards and groats
2 potatoes and point to absent meat; a meatless day
3 a good feed after killing a pig
4 stare
5 to peep, look
6 glower
7 look closely
8 hard labouring work
9 hardworking, capable
10 a fit of laziness
11 quite good
12 clothes basket
13 light bag for shopping
14 dry, wither (of vegetation)
15 stye on the eye
16 cheeky; over-sexed
17 blundering; tactless
18 go very fast
19 go very fast like the mail coach
20 miserable-looking bird, a winter migrant
21 melancholy, wretched
22 chattering jays
23 properly
24 to drag the feet
25 to drink greedily
26 upright post to which a bullock was tied in a stall
27 stone mushroom acting as part of corn rick's base
28 over-cooked; badly cooked
29 the smell of burning
30 knock and break
31 smithereens
32 conduits; drains

A DIALECT ALPHABET

Aglets are berries on a hawthorn tree bough,
Bottoms are valleys untouched by the plough.
Crib's a mid-morning snack, going down good,
Durn is a door-frame that's made out of wood.
Evil's a fork, for spreading out dung,
Fernaigue's to deceive, by act or by tongue.
Gaddling means drinking as fast as you can,
A *hibbledehoy* is between boy and man.
Iles are the beards that on barley are seen,
Jig means a mockery of God or the Queen.
Keeve is a big tub for salting a pig,
Things 'teared all to *lerrups*' are not very big.
A *mincher* is one who escapes out of school,
A *new vang* is new, but won't last as a rule.
Ovees is a word for the eaves of a roof,
Paddick's a small pitcher; not breakage proof.
Q is a *Quailaway*, a stye on the eye,
River is any small stream that runs by.
There are two words for scratch, to *sclum* and to *sclow*,
T is a *tich-pipe* – 'Let's have a smoke now.'
Ugly describes your bad temper, not looks,
Veer is a farrow; one that still sucks.
W is *wisht* when things badly are done,
X is for *zackly* without the 'x' on.
Y is for *yorks* to keep trouser-legs clean,
Z for *zam-zoodled*, half-baked, poor cuisine.
There are twenty-six letters in dialect too;
Here's a number of words that are Cornish for you.

A SENSE OF DIRECTION

We Rochers do go *in* St Columb
And *in* St Austell too.
We may even go *down* Bugle
When there's nothing better to do.

We generally go *over* St Dennis,
Out Padstow and *back* Lockengate,
Up Plymouth, *up* Exeter, *up* London,
Though the way be crooked or straight.

'*Upwards* he's gone, where times is brisk'
Was a phrase from old folks' speech;
But *downwards*, mostly, to the sea –
Down Newquay, and *down* beach.

A city set upon a hill
Cannot be hid, they say.
So people from Withiel and St Wenn
Go *up* Roche, any day.

But if we live near Hensbarrow,
At Greensplatt, say, on the down,
We go *down* Roche, as to a place
Of culture and renown.

Now all this fine sense of direction
Will disappear at one scat;
We shall all start to go *to* everywhere,
And that, I suppose, will be that.

THE VISITOR

NOT much is recorded about Roche in the eighteenth century. A cold winter might decrease the population; a warm summer a few months later might increase it. But in 1768, somebody did arrive.

The Reverend Samuel Furly
In seventy sixty-eight,
Was Rector of Roche parish,
A good man early and late.
He never had need of a church bell,
For his lungs were mighty and stout;
Boanerges the people called him,
Son of thunder, a great man to shout.

Word came up from Meager at Medrose
Over Luxulyan way;
An important preacher was coming,
Would arrive that very day.
Sam Furly was 'some bustled up'.
There's no company hereabout.
"I better tell cook get a dinner on
And give the boy a shout."

His wife said "Sam, you'm a worthy man
And this John is a friend to thee,
So we'll do our best." But Sam replied
"I can't come up to he;
He say that the world is his parish
And he mean it I don't doubt.
I've got all I can manage in Roche,
With all my bluster and shout."

We don't know what they talked of
In Roche that September day.
'Twas 'a comfortable evening'
Is all the records say.
Sam Furly and John Wesley,
Two good men and devout,
In the comfort of that evening
Neither had need to shout.

Sam Furley and John Wesley
Have gone to their reward
But there's something in tradition
And certain things die hard,
For whether they're in the claywork,
Carr'ing hay or falling out,
They still keep up Sam's custom:
Roche people d'always shout.

Details of John Wesley's visit to Roche are given in *The Wesleys in Cornwall* by John Pearce.

THE MISER

READING H. M. Creswell Payne's *The Story of the Parish of Roche* (p.78) I came upon the following note:

'The sister of Mr John Keen (a noted surgeon) married a Phillipps of Rosemellin, and carried her brother's wealth into the family. Of the Phillipps family two were rectors of the adjoining parish of Lanivet; there is a tradition that during the Civil War the family plate was buried in one of the brakes at Rosemellin, and never afterwards recovered.'

Several years ago now, in the company of a friend with a metal detector, we ran over the more accessible parts of Rosemellin in a vain search for what Creswell Payne calls 'the treasure of the Phillipps family'. In response to the bleeps of the gadget, we found the top of a marmalade jar and a metal milk churn label. It occurs to me that history might repeat itself . . .

I began farming Lower Penstrase
Since nineteen thirty-two.
Nothing much on back in they days
And whacks of work to do.

I kep' on farming through the war –
A reserved occupation.
I killed a pig every *whip and while*[1]
And never minded the rations.

I got a grant for to plough the down,
And subsidies beside.
'Twouldn' do to refuse the money
What the government provide.

A *wisht*[2] hand I was at the cooking
And all that women's trade.
Mrs Bunt up the road used to say to me
"What you need is a *maid*.[3]"

But the maids their eyes was elsewhere
On good-looking chaps and that.
(Half of they chaps is now divorced,
And several have gone *scat*.[4])

With peace, the milk-cheques rolling in
Kep' the wolf from the door.
Well, kep' the wolf a brave way off,
But for the taxman I was poor.

*   *   *

'Twas good I had spare milk churns
To keep the money in.
No matter the passon told me
That avarice was a sin!

And now that 'm beating on a bit
What do I do with the cash?
I don't want to spend it all to once,
And I couldn't do anything rash.

I could go down to the pub, I s'pose
And spend a bit in drinkin',
But I was brought up Band of Hope
And am still that way of thinkin'.

I could give some to the chapel,
But the chapel's 'bout gone in.
They'm down to only two families now –
Everyone kith and kin.

Old Granny Bunt (not a tooth in her head)
Says "A Cause is what you need,
You haven't got *no chick nor cheeld*[5],
You've never had mouths to feed."

I never heeard such nonsense –
'Tis against all Nature's laws.
All that *lowster*[6] and all that sweat,
Only for some good cause –

I know what I'll do; I'll bury it
Over Rosemellin Moor.

Nobody but me'll know where 'tis to,
Or what 'tis over there for.

Years to come, some scholar chap
(With a curly pipe) will appear;
"Traditions of treasure on Rosemellin Moor
Are entirely bogus, I fear".

So my money will all be unhurted,
My investment's good for sure;
They'll be buried deep in Rosemellin,
And safe for ever more.

1 every so often   4 gone bankrupt
2 very bad   5 no offspring
3 girl-friend   6 hard labouring work

RADIX MALORUM

ANOTHER set of verses on a subject dear to the heart of most Cornish men and women: money. I must have been about twelve years old when I was advised by a clay-captain's wife, no less: "Well, Kenneth, we read in the Bible that money is the root of all evil; but yet I always think that a little of it is handy." The phrase stuck in my memory, and has produced the following:

> I come of a saving family
> And my husband is saving too;
> We never thrawed anything away,
> But managed with making do.
> We never spent very much on drink
> (Though I kip a drop of brandy)
> For money's the root of all evil for sure
> But a little of it is handy.
>
> Mother would say "Now then you maids
> See that you mind your needle!
> We need to patch and darn things up."
> We were never allowed to wheedle
> Our way into any *flam-new*[1] clothes,
> Have jewellery, sweets or candy.
> Money was the root of all evil,
> Though a little might be handy.
>
> When Anniversary time comed round
> We maids used to feel some dowdy:
> Everybody else dressed up to the nines,
> And wearing their new clothes proudly.

Mother said "Chapel's no place for *flinks*[2]
And I think they maids look randy.
Read what Paul say of money and that
(Though a little of it is handy)."

'Twadn' long before my sister Jane
Had fixed herself up with a man:
"I'm leaving this scroungy place," she said,
"So soon as ever I can.
I know Jake's a bit *foreright*[3] in the house
And his legs is a little bit bandy,
But he done all right from his father's will
And a little money is handy."

Now what I done didn't please at all.
I fall'd for our neighbour's son.
We wudn' on speaking terms with they
Which was fullish when all's said and done.
"I don't *shake no straws*[4] with that lot," said Pa,
"He can go to the Rio Grande!
Besides, what's he bringing along with hisself? –
A little money'd be handy."

Well, the jist of it was, I married Ted,
After three years of rows alarming.
We started up in our own little place –
Pa called it 'wheelbarrow farming'.
We was *brave and poor*[5] for a year or two
Though, as Ted was never a dandy
And never spent very much on clothes,
That money came in handy.

I do tell my maids "You must work your stint
And value what you've got.
And you'll have a place as good as mine –
At least, as like as not."
For though we read in the Good Book
(I do keep it next to the brandy)
That money's the root of all evil for sure
Yet a little of it – just a little of it –
A little of it is handy.

1 brand new   3 blundering, clumsy   5 rather poor
2 meretricious display 4 having no dealings

KNUCKLY-DOWNS

THE tradition of the knuckly down is still probably not quite dead. A. L. Rowse recalls his father saying "In Roche they do knuckly down 'pon one knee". Even within the last twenty years an elderly St Dennis man refused to come to Roche to live, giving as the reason: "I don't want to go up there among they old knuckly-downs". Dr Rowse suggests sexual undertones to the phrase; but I give here the more decorous version I learnt.

We Rochers went over St Dennis
To a church service 'do' held up there;
'Twas a lot of bowing and scraping
And everything up in the air.

We Rochers bain't ceremonious,
We'm down-to-earth, come what may.
There's they that consider we'm *foreright*[1],
Which means wanting in tact, as they say.

'Twas a *new vang*[2] with St Dennis
And showing they'm up with the nobs:
They had bells and the smells of incense;
'Twas one of they High Church jobs.

I suppose we wud'n doing it zackly,
We was rather confused, I don't doubt,
But we got to a point in the service
When a man from St Dennis called out:

20

"*Knuckly* [3] down, all ye Rochers;
Take and do the same as we.
And don't clutter up the aisles and the pews
And the chancel and gallery."

'Twas years and generations ago
But the name and the fame have stuck.
'Knuckly-downs' we have been ever since,
 I s'pose it is just our luck.

But a witty Roche man was inspired
As he looked at St Dennis Moor;
"*Sloany-pie* [4] is all's to eat here."
And that too became the folk lore.

So "sloany-pie" and "knuckly-downs"
Were the battle-cries over the moors.
Backalong [5], of course, they'd *be fightable* [6]
But we've come to the end of those wars.

For what is the point of localities
Fighting for local renown,
When all we do do is join forces
For another straggly town?

1 blundering	3 kneel	5 in the past
2 novelty	4 fruit pie made with sloes	6 prepare to fight

THE BETROTHAL

I haven't seen you for ages
Have you been busy too?
We've had some *pant*[1] up our place
A proper *randyvoo*[2].

'Tis 'long of our boy, William John
Inviting home his maid.
Talked to her like a sister,
He wud'n a bit dismayed.

Course, I was *cutting up a bit*[3] –
'Twudn' do to talk too broad;
Though, for some up-the-country piece
I wudn' be overawed.

Last Sunday, they went to chapel;
The people there made some fuss,
They half shaked poor Lucy's hand off
And said she was 'one of us'.

We'd a handsome dinner the Sunday –
Two pullets I'd brought on.
Well, I had to do the best I could
For my boy, William John.

I *made meanings*[4] to father
When the meal was nearly done.
He had took out his pipe to *smuckie*[5]
But I stopped 'un before he'd begun.

Lucy's colours went up a little
When Father said "Let's see this bad cow."
They went to the cows' house to *drunch*[6] her
And of course, the maid didn't know how!

But she showed herself brave and useful
When she got the knack of the drunch.
"She's some *keenly*[7] maid," said Father,
"Sure 'nough, she's the best of the bunch!"

"If I was you boy," said he after,
"I'd clinch the deal here and now."
So I think that's what John'll be doing
Best thing, I'm sure you'll allow.

So that's why I been so busy,
And bustled up, you can guess.
But I hope John'll put the question
And Lucy will answer 'Yes'.

---

1 panic
2 social occasion

3 talking in a refined
  manner
4 made signs

5 smoke
6 dose with cattle medicine
7 capable

THE AUCTION SALE

FIFTY years ago, auction sales often occurred in dwelling houses, and were much liked by the inquisitive, who would *nawse in* (nose in). The following account is not entirely fictitious, some details being taken from an auction described in Charles Lee's *Journal*. I was also recalling a sale in a house where a sofa seemed not to sell. My father called out to the auctioneer, a Mr Stanley Marshall, "I'm just goin' next door a minute; if he's not sold 'gin I get back I'll give 'ee ninepence for'n." He got the sofa at that figure.

Whatever be'ee buying they *joneys*[1] fur,
Filling the house with *trade*[2]?
Queen Victoria's nawse knocked off
From the time that she was made.

By goles!, an American organ,
What will you do with 'ee?
Goin' t'have a Sankey evening
In society?

And now you've bid for three old hens –
A mercy you've lost that lot –
Take six weeks to boil and a fortnight to ait,
Be thankful for what you ain't got.

Now what do 'ee want with lead piping?
No use to man or beast,
And probably stealed from the old church roof –
Or perished to say the least.

And look at the guff they'm throwin' down
From over the bedroom sills.
Look at the *stewer*³ that's rising up,
And the smill – as old as the hills.

Tenpence is cheap for a sofa,
You'm right there, I must say,
But not when he got one leg falled off
And springs out every way.

I could do good with a kettle,
But not with a rusty spout.
You can *put the best side toward London*⁴
But the water got to come out.

Now come home for a bite to eat;
You'm getting carried away.
You ain't safe to go to auction sales.
I don't think we'd better stay.

1 ornaments, especially Staffordshire figures
2 stuff   3 dust
4 put the best aspect on a not very promising job

RECOGNITION

SOME of us are alert, following Daphne du Maurier's *Vanishing Cornwall*, to Cornish idiosyncrasies; and I think this may be one. I have known more than one person get *vitty hurried* (very annoyed) as we say, if the listener does not instantly recognise a person mentioned in an anecdote, whom the speaker considers should be known: "How don't 'ee knaw'n? You must knaw'n!"

> I knaw what I was goin' tell you,
> When I sid you again –
> You knaw that fellow Davey
> What live down Carbis Lane –
>
> Well - what d'ee mean you don't knaw'n?
> You've seen un around the lanes –
> He used to work for the Council,
> Cleaning the cunderds and drains.
>
> He done a little bit with moleskins,
> But that was before the war;
> They done what they could back in they days,
> When people was brave and poor.
>
> I can't think how you don't knaw 'un –
> He used to sell turnips by night.
> He used to come round with a handcart –
> Singing with all his might.

You must knaw his cousin, Aunt Dinah,
Looked so *taissy*'s* a snake,
Clouted the kids' heads up chapel
To make sure they kep' awake.

Giddaway do! – you knaw 'un;
His mother and yours swapped cats.
You must be a bit of relation –
Have 'ee ever thought about that?

You won't admit that you knaw 'un
However hard I've tried.
I suppose it don't really matter now –
The poor fella's just up and died!

* irritable, bad-tempered

DOG DANCING

The old folks called it dog dancing:
Fooling round to nobody's benefit.
Those *hibbledehoys*[1], whether girls or boys,
Were all of them tackled with '*better fit*'[2].

Better fit you go and clean the cunderds,
Better fit you help to turn the hay.
Better fit you swot the flies (there's hundreds)
Better than foolin' around any day.
Better fit you go and whitewash the cows-house,
Better fit you mend that gate with a *trig*[3].
Better fit you pick they fowls for the boiler,
Better fit you help to kill the pig.

But what of the modern dog dancing –
Scatting[4] up kiosks and such?
Better fit they done something useful –
Or is that asking too much?

Better fit they seen the other person's viewpoint,
Better fit they counted the cost of it all.
Better fit their hair looked less like a *vuzz-rick*[5],
Better fit they turned down the row in the Hall.

    Or is 'better fit' a way for we oldies
To make the young do what we want them to do?
    Better fit we thought of the time, backalong,
We was bored and *ballyragged*[6] and fed up too.

1 youths and maidens, not fully adult
2 it would be better if . . .
3 wedge

4 breaking up
5 rick of furze
6 abused

NEWQUAY

Newquay. In the thirties,
And evening coming in.
Young men and maids, in full evening dress –
Swallow tails, and waistline thin.
The bettermost class of people
Out for an evening's spree. But
"Come on. Back to the station.
'Tis not for the likes of we."

Newquay. In the nineties,
The young in teenage guise
Like 'an owl looking out of an ivy-bush'
With their hair around their eyes.
No problem now who own the place
For everyone can see,
That Newquay in the nineties
Is full of the likes of we.

- HE DO PURDLY LOOK AFTER HIS MOTHER -

MY friend, Dr John Rowe of Luxulyan, has suggested that the test
of a thriving dialect is that it can be used for serious subjects and
is not purely a source of humour. The following is an attempt at
a serious dialect poem:

> He do *purdly*[1] look after his mother.
> But she had a hard time of it once;
> Bringing up that little *come-by-chance*[2]
> Made in some courtyard or *caunce*[3].
>
> The father went over the ocean,
> Never showed face here no more.
> Left the poor boy in our village.
> That was before the war.
>
> No Social back in they days.
> You managed how you could.
> And she wouldn't go on the parish
> For the pride was in her blood.
>
> 'Twas her pride that kept her going,
> A credit I must say.
> She took in washing and sewing
> And went charring every day.
>
> Her boy should want for nothing –
> Pocket-money, the lot.
> New suit for Anniversary –
> He looked after what he got.

And he purdly looked after his mother.
Now there's well-brought up grandchildren too.
Her boy do like things regular
After what he have been through.

"These things are sent for a purpose,"
The old folks used to say.
And purpose, with hard struggle
Can bring a better day.

1 an expression of approval
2 illegitimate child
3 paved courtyard

HAY-TIME

When I see swiss rolls drawn by tractors
Blocking up the way,
And am told 'tis rolls of silage
Or else rolls of hay;

I recall how years ago now
In the summer weather,
We'd all go and turn the hay up,
Everyone together.

I seem to hear the voices calling
"A bit more will do the trick,
For over here the hay is handsome
But down there 'tis green's a *lick*[1]."

"Oo look there, oo there's a *wilky*[2];
Now we can tell the weather;
Sunshine if he's yellow and bright,
Rain if he's dull like leather."

"I'm sure I don't know what'll happen –
They clouds full's egg over there.
If we get much rain like last evening
The farmer will be in some *tear*[3]."

Well, all 'tis, we'll have to *pooky*[4] –
Pook it all up from the *drams*[5].
Shame, we got so near to carr'in,
No use all the swears and damns."

John's time *to make the hay sweet*[6]
Twists some straw around Sue's neck,
Catch her in a shady corner
And Sue offers him no check.

So the tractors, roaring onward,
Don't impress me with their noise.
I still see the old-style hayfield
With its trials and its joys.

1 leek
2 frog
3 rage
4 put into haycocks
5 swathes of grass, as they fall from the mower
6 custom of kissing in the hayfield

THE BIG BANG

'Twas after Germany's collapse
And victory, too, against the Japs
We Rochers thought 'Well now, perhaps
We'll have a celebration
Like others of our nation.'

But where do 'ee let off fireworks to?
In Roche, the decision's easy, you –
The Rock, from below there's a handsome view –
Or from down Rock Lane hallooin'
To all the echoing ruin.

As darkness comed late one summer day
Crowds of villagers made their way
A firework show for to survey,
In keen anticipation
Of firework observation.

Two, 'head and chief,' on the Rock did show
But a third man stayed in the cell below.
He thought that with fireworks 'twas touch and go.
He would avoid the option
Of having some *confloption*[1]!

One of the three on the top had *frecked*[2]
Some shovel-hilts to launch rockets erect
All of them carefully circumspect,
So any conflagration
Should be in moderation.

Rockets went up, to "ooh" and "ah",
And falled among many a falling star;
It all seemed very regular.
But a *mismeant*[3] upon the venture fell –
Some sparks come down in the hermit's cell.

A noise, a rumble, a mighty roar:
Was it Tregeagle, so black as a craw,
Who'd got something chucking him in his maw?
(For indigestion is an evil
Whether it do fall on man or devil.)

Tregeagle has had a shocking press,
From pillar to post he's had no rest,
But ballyragged everywhere here in the West;
Till at last in shock,
He got stuck in Roche Rock.

But this lot wud'n Tregeagle at all,
'Twas exploding fireworks from sparks let fall
And the third man there waiting, to fear in thrall,
Skiddered down the iron ladder
Like a skeiner[4], only sadder.

'Twas discovered though, I fear,
The Roche big bang had cost them dear –
And questions asked both far and near:
What were the committee doin'
To be the cause of total ruin?

A village wit who was standing by
Said "Russian aeroplanes on the spy
Photographed they shovel-hilts from the sky;
Though Roche's fireworks might be aimless
The village ain't exactly fameless!"

1 flurry
2 arranged fussily
3 mishap
4 (to go) very fast

MRS TABB

AS life became a little more prosperous in the nineteen-thirties, it became the thing in Roche to buy a piano and pay for a music teacher; in Roche this was probably Mrs Tabb. She trained three generations of proficient musicians, being a most competent teacher.

An electrician's wife and a teacher of music,
Letters after her name, and a family what's more;
About twice as busy as most of her neighbours,
Walking for three steps and running for four.

With a "wrong in your bass," and a "wrong in your tenor;
And *librato*, that means let the piano go free –
And now just a minute, I must see to the fishcakes
That I'm cooking up in time for Sam's tea!"

And the cost of all this? Fifteen shillings a quarter.
Just three pound a year to open the door
To Handel and Schubert and Bach and Beethoven
And Elgar and goodness knows how many more.

With a "wrong in your bass, and you'm right in your tenor!
Allargando, that means just as grand as can be.
You wait there a minute, I must see to the fishcakes,
That I'm getting ready when Sam come for his tea!"

If you were to hear her, on a tinny piano
Coax little singers performing alone,
Or turning rumbustious for some noisy tenor
Who needs a big noise that matches his own!

"You'm wrong in your bass, and you'm wrong in your tenor.
Andante, that means that the going is slow.
Well there, never mind; the fishcakes are ready;
Wrap up this cold weather; 'tis time for to go!"

Trezaise chapel organ, and Widor's *Toccata*
Who would think those two could possibly join?
Yet she did it, with taste and technique on occasion;
That organ will never again sound so fine.

"You'm right in your bass, and oh yes, that's better.
Finito, that means that's 'bout 'nough for today.
So see you next Tuesday – my goodness, the fishcakes!
Oh dear I shall have to throw this lot away!"

Dear Mrs Tabb; what else can I tell you?
You belong to those people who know how to teach.
You gave musical knowledge to three generations.
Your watchword was practice, rather than preach.
With exams and with contests, with sheer inspiration,
You earned for yourself the best kind of fame.
And as those that you taught would most certainly testify
You earned every letter comes after your name.

A short time before she died, in 1997, Mrs Tabb received the MBE.
The process of recommendation for that honour was started and
co-ordinated by Ken, though he himself died before the award was
officially announced.

P.R.P.

ON NOT TEARIN' NOTHIN' UP

There's a trustee meeting up chapel tonight,
So we got to keep lively for that.
If we leave the weeds *quail*[1] *'gin*[2] tomorrow
I don't s'pose we'll zackly go *scat*[3].

Passon say, if we want it
We can have the churchyard hay,
But I think we'll leave it go quiet
And not tear nothin' up – not today.

There's a lamb on tiddy-bottle
That you really ought to see;
Here he is. Idn' he handsome?
Oops – not yet standing free.

That dear chield that you'm holdin'
I dare say I know by a sweet.
Come over to me then, my lover,
We'll have something nice for to eat.

Well, of course, we still got to watch points,
And see that we ain't sold a pup.
But 'tis brave and hot, and we got the *larr*[4]
So I don't think we'll tear nothin' up.

1 wither
2 till

3 bankrupt
4 a fit of laziness

TAKEN DOWN A PEG, OR,
ST WENN COUNCIL HOUSES

'POETRY is the spontaneous overflow of powerful feelings; it takes its origin from emotion recollected in tranquillity.' Thus Wordsworth; and here am I, forty years after the conversation recorded below, tranquilly repeating the details of an encounter on the Goss Moor that at the time aroused such strong feelings of annoyance that even the resources of the Cornish dialect were strained to represent: 'teassy', 'fitty hurried', 'up ninety', 'in some tear', 'maazed', etc.

> I was passing St Wenn council houses
> At the end of a long summer day;
> I had gone for a walk on the Goss Moors,
> And met someone I knew midway.

> My Auntie Louie was standing
> In minatory, monitory wise.
> She looked like a prophetess of old
> With her beret pulled over her eyes.

"Well, I s'pose you won't be an expense now,
To your poor old mam and dad.
So you've got yourself a job at last;
They'll both of 'em be some glad.

"Well, where be 'ee goin' teach? Up Nottingham?
What's wrong with the schools round here?
I don't know what you'm doing up Nottingham
When you might have tried somewhere near."

She paused; as a cat gives a mouse a chance
To breathe till a second blow.
Then: "You don't *go in 'cross no wrasslin'*[1] s'pose.
'Twould keep 'ee fit, you know.

"My boys" (there were five) "have all won the belt
For wrasslin', different places,
And Billy, the best of 'em, just 'bout thrawed
Sid Chapman over the traces!"

I pondered over this mighty feat.
It seemed my claim to renown
Was, my cousin had picked Sid Chapman up
And had (just 'bout) put'n down.

I walked home from St Wenn council houses
A sadder, wiser man.
Face to face with Auntie Louie
Things had not gone according to plan.

Back home, I told my annoyance,
My anger and misery.
"Everyone of Louie's boys is a shift-boss[2],"
Said mother reproachfully.

1 go in for (Cornish) wrestling
2 a position of some authority in the clay industry

WE LOVE THE PLACE

As spoken by a widow of eighty

I do like to go chapel early
And sit in my own pew.
I can relax there lovely
Like my mother used to do.

I been coming here over seventy years –
'Twas here I met my man
And now he's gone I keep comin'
As regular as I can.

The weeks go by so quickly now –
A moment, and they'm gone.
But I know I shall see father again
When my time down here is done.

Sometimes, as I sit, my mind runs back
To old Cap'n Arthur's days:
I hear him shouting out "Glowry!"
And "Give to the Lord the praise!"

Once Captain Arthur caught we maids
Hanging 'round outside the door.
He *raced us up*[1] outside the porch,
And my goodness he give we what for.

He was every inch the clay cap'n,
With his stick he angrily taps:
"You maids come here to worship God
And not to be seen by the chaps!"

That was umpteen years and years ago,
'Tis wisht to dwell on the past –
I've seen they flowers up here before,
I should never have thought they would last.

Now, here comes the chapel steward
Fixing the hymn-board on.
I must say I dearly love singing hymns
Though it *minds*² me of days that are gone.

There's lots of new hymns that's going round now –
For guitars and these tubular bells;
But I like 'We love the place O God
Wherein thine honour dwells'.

I've done some caretaking in this place,
Now we can't afford to employ.
I've brished and I've scrubbed and I've dusted;
It wasn't always a joy.

I've helped to distemper these acres of walls
Till I was all but ready to faint,
But we had some fun when Boysie Bewes
Kicked over a tin of paint.

I've even stoked up the boiler
To help on a public tea.
'Course, now we do switch on the 'lectric.
'Tis heaps more convenient, see?

Ah, here come the little *tackers*³
Toddling down the aisle.

47

One of them turn hisself around
And he look to me, and he smile.

'Suffer the little children
And forbid them not,' He said.
You do get *maze*[4] with 'em sometimes;
But without them, 'twould be some dead.

Here's the preacher, in a new black coat –
He never got that on tick.
He's a schoolteacher in to Bodmin.
I should think he was brave and strict.

He is giving out the hymn number,
And the organ behind him swells.
Oh *handsome*[5]! – 'We love the place O God
Wherein Thine honour dwells'.

'The widow of eighty' was Ken's mother and the chapel, of
course, was Trezaise. Trezaise Chapel closed in April 2001, its
passing mourned particularly by those families who for
generations had been so closely associated with it.

P.R.P.

1 arranged us in order
2 reminds us
3 toddlers
4 cross, annoyed
5 lovely

A PRAYER TO MY ANCESTORS

Forgers and finders of ways,
With hearts too strong for your heads,
Who knew that the self betrays
When indiscretion leads;

Who localised your hope,
And legalised your lust,
In cob-walled tabernacles
Established all your trust;

Who kept your anger righteous,
And saved your fear for the Lord,
Were wise in your generation,
And eloquent for the Word;

Grant me your parsimony,
You wise deployment give,
That anger and lust and fear
May all help me to live.

POLLUTION

THE following verse was a prize-winner in a *Spectator* competition of 1972. Entries were invited on some 'disturbing manifestations of pollution' and English China Clays had just published their long-term plans for the clay area: Roche had been designated an 'island settlement' in the midst of 'micaceous residue'. Although much has since been done to reduce pollution by the china clay industry, in view of recent (2001) plans for the siting of refuse incinerators in the Roche area, it still seems relevant.

P.R.P.

The streams have all been poisoned, and the rivers now run
    white,
But come to sunny Cornwall, and revel in the blight.
Only, if you choose mid-Cornwall, we'd advise that you
    make haste;
The villages are being swamped in seas of sandy waste.
They now call them 'island settlements', the County
    planners' name;
It is clay-workers who've settled there; they're obviously fair
    game,
And china-clay earns dollars, so who are we to grouse?
(The Company will pay them when they bulldoze down
    their house.)
As you gaze o'er churned-up slag-heaps on a semi-lunar
    land,
You can read the 'long-term strategy' for all the mess
    they've planned.
Mounds of 'micaceous residue' in hectares and in acres,
(Since we're going into Europe, land can go to 'any takers')

And if it's planned at County Hall, of course it must be right,
(What they're doing to mid-Cornwall is done from a great height).

As for ourselves, our bungalow looks straight across the Channel,
So we really do not mind if people foul the Hayle or Gannel.
But what's this? Men in gas-masks? Toxic oil-drums on the shore?
Oh, let's get back to London; I can't stand it any more!

AUNTIE HANNAH

"When you grow up and write a book, Kenneth,"
Said my aunt to me as I toddled after,
Helping her feed the hens, "You will have to call
Fowls' dung, chickens' droppings." It was always so.
A sheltered, filtered life she led, but it wasn't easy,
As she scoured the pans and the food
Free from injurious matter as her mind.
Her drink came strained through the Western Temperance
    League.
(She bought me their journal, *The Clarion*, 'for Western
    wide-awakes')
Her fiction *The Sunday Companion*, and the fourpenny
    Christian novels,
And her view of the world from the chaste columns
Of the *Western Morning News*.
Even the Bible she read in bits, through the Scripture
    Union,
And she took it, as prescribed. "For there are bad words
In the Bible, Kenneth, but we do not need to read them."
And sex was the memory of a soldier, killed in the
    trenches,
And never mentioned after but with a tearful eye.

*　　*　　*

She is dead now, long ago; and perhaps it is well,
For what would she make of a wife-swapping world,
And the chapels turned into chip-shops, and a strip-tease act
In the very room where they once held the District Synod?

*　　*　　*

I can see her still, of a Sunday, come home from morning
    chapel
And putting her hat, with the hatpin stuck in it sideways,
Back on the sideboard, ready for evening service,
And patting her sidecombs straight. "What was the text then,
    Kenneth?
I bet you can't remember." – "Yes, I can, Auntie Hannah."
(You might get a sweet for that.)

             *   *   *

Her grave has a white stone, and decent marble chippings.
And I pray that she still may rest in quiet,
Where pornographers cease from troubling,
And the prudish are at rest.

FRED

On the last bus to home,
On the last, the friendliest seat,
Sits Fred, drunk as a lord,
Through drinking brandy, neat.

With a weird and quavering voice
And breaths that are short and wheezy
He sings 'The miner's dream
Of home' and 'Daisy, Daisy'.

Drawn through his toothless mouth,
Out of his empty gums,
Down through the rocketing bus
The toneless whining comes.

The women purse their lips
When his wild music starts;
Draw close their decent skirts
And button up their hearts.

Only the men look back
In wry appreciation,
That of the dregs of life
He pours this last libation.

MR AXWORTHY

"I've brought your mother some beans."
Dressed in a once-best suit of navy serge
Now green with age, he hobbles forward
Tendering his offering in bony arms.
"Roche is no place for beans. 'Tis cold here,
The soil's poor. Trevaunance, now,
That was the place for beans. You could grow
Handsome stuff. For fifty years
I've worked there, man and boy,
In they huge gardens, and weeding the drives and paths,
Mister, you couldn't see a weed, not nowhere.
Many's the time, when folks was off on charabangs,
Down to the beach or wherever, August Bank Holiday,
I would say, 'Ladyship, I must do the drive.'
'Axworthy,' she'd say, 'Don't you ever want a holiday?'
'Your ladyship,' I'd answer, 'Haven't I always
Spent all my time doing the gardens? Haven't I now?'
'Axworthy,' she'd say, 'You have.' "
He shuffles off, coping with new-found freedoms,
And heart heavy from viewing wider horizons.

A GRAMMAR OF INTEGRITY

If is the way of condition,
The junction, conjunction of hope and regret,
And, in the main, disaster.
The academic cul-de-sac, the inhuman dream,
The bovine bovarism;
The dark eyes, invitingly restrained.
If the glue had been stronger, the sun had shone weaker,
If the sights had been adjusted, the senses alerted.
The heart whole in humility –
But by *if* fell Icarus.

While is the temporal, and the temporary,
The devil may care, and will!
The kettle a-simmer,
The watched crock, waiting for the diversion.
The comptometer counting the countless faults.
While the sophisticate fiddles, the porter dozes,
The rat gnaws at the roof-tree –
By *while* Rome burns.

Though is the turn of the tide, the restoration.
Adversative to adversity.
The sail set to the wind, the biceps trained for strain,
The husbanded desire, the thrift of promise
In a catchpenny life.
Though the guard was heavy, the trance deadly in depth,
The night drear, with dwindling stars –
By *though* was the stone moved.

DEVIOUS WAYS

"You do not trust me, do you?"
You said, and I answered "No".
And even as we spoke the words
Our eyes knew it was not so.

Oh, better far than politeness,
Skimming the ice of convention
Is the banter of an insult
Warmed by a loving intention.

For kindliness, in devious ways
Can use quarrelsome words, or none,
And the depth of a love which may find no words
Can be read in discrepant tone.

A BIBLE CHRISTIAN CHAPEL

Oh, love that will not let me go –
I trace thee in the pattern of the aisle,
I see thee in the lilies' brazen show,
And know thee in the steward's lustrous smile.

Oh light, that lightenest all my days –
The coloured glass reflects thee in the pew,
The stuttering lamp yields thee its borrowed ray,
And the glossy varnish, making all things new.

Oh joy, that reachest me through pain,
Oh beauty that in drabness finds its scope,
Oh spirit, husbanded in years of gain,
That for lean years vouchsafest a solvent hope.

If there is any God, these men will know,
Who guide with courage and who guard with fear,
Their short, yet strong tradition of Heaven's glow.
If there is any God, He will be here!

ON A CORNISH CHURCH IN WINTER

The branches, winding through the silver sky
Involve the silent tower in mystery.
This is the granite time, when winds at strife
Exact an apathy from all gentler life.
Now may we see, as after fire and flood,
It is the stone that lives, and not the wood.
Oh miracle of man, when roots of stone
Thrust up such branches, with the air at one.